THE HOFFNUNG
SYMPHONY ORCHESTRA

By the Author of
THE MAESTRO

The

Hoffnung

Symphony Orchestra

by
Gerard Hoffnung

London: Dennis Dobson

First Published March 1955
Second Impression June 1955
Third Impression (revised edition) November 1955
Fourth Impression February 1957
Fifth Impression October 1957
Sixth Impression June 1958

I would like to express my thanks to Messrs.
Bradbury, Agnew & Co., Ltd., proprietors of
PUNCH, and to Hulton Press Ltd., for publishing
in advance some of the drawings in this book. GH

Published in Great Britain in 1955 *by Dobson Books Ltd.*
80 *Kensington Church Street, London, W.*8

Printed by Chas. Pearson & Son Ltd., London

THE STRINGS

The Violin (Leader)

The Violon Double

The Viola

The Viola Pizzicato

The Yo-Bow

The Cello

The Double Bass (a left handed player)

13

The Piccolo Double Bass

The Harp

15

The String Tuba

This instrument is sometimes referred to as the "Minstrel Tuba" or the "Blow-Plucker". It is interesting to note that the String Tuba is a member of both the string and brass families though it is usually seated with the former.

The Zither

The Piano (Boudoir Grand)

The Spanish Guitar

The Ondes Martenot

THE WOODWIND

THE WOODEND

The Flute and the Piccolo Flute

23

The Bass Flute

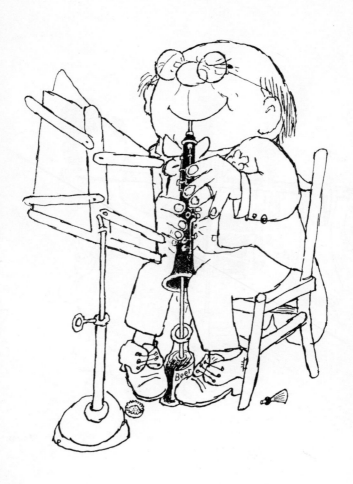

The Oboe

26

The Cor Anglais

The Heckle-Phone

28

The Clarinet and the Bass Clarinet

29

The Saxophone

The Bassethorn

The Bassoon

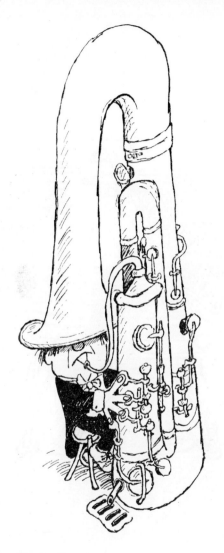

The Contra-Bassoon

The Organ

THE BRASS

The Horn

The Trinkler

The Double Trumpet

The Serpent

For security reasons this instrument
is no longer in use.

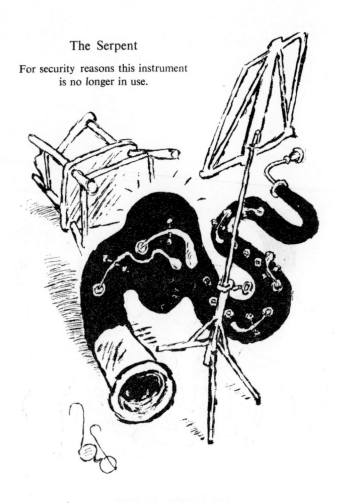

The Trombone

The Bass Trombone

The Wagner Tuba

The Bass Tuba

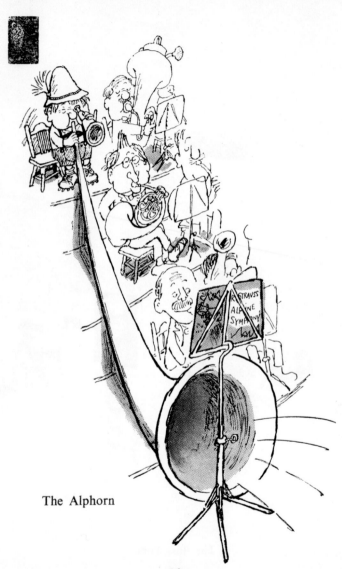

The Alphorn

THE PERCUSSION

The Timpani

49

The Cymbals

The Side Drum

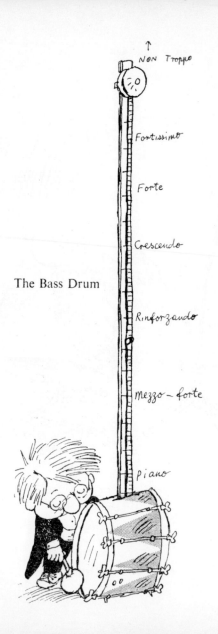

The Bass Drum

The Tum Drum

The Tubular Bells

The Triangle

The Xylophone

The Vibraphone

The Celeste

The Jingle Bells and the Chinese Block

The Wind Machine

The Gong and the Tam Tam

The Castanets

THE
END.

INDEX

	Page
The Violin	7
The Violon Double	8
The Viola	9
The Viola Pizzicato	10
The Yo-Bow	11
The 'Cello	12
The Double Bass	13
The Piccolo Double Bass	14
The Harp	15
The String Tuba	16
The Zither	17
The Piano	18
The Spanish Guitar	19
The Ondes Martenot	20
The Flute and the Piccolo Flute	23
The Bass Flute	24 & 25
The Oboe	26
The Cor Anglais	27
The Heckle-Phone	28
The Clarinet and the Bass Clarinet	29
The Saxophone	30
The Bassethorn	31
The Bassoon	32
The Contra-Bassoon	33
The Organ	34
The Horn	37
The Trinkler	38
The Double Trumpet	39
The Serpent	40
The Trombone	41
The Bass Trombone	42 & 43
The Wagner Tuba	44
The Bass Tuba	45
The Alphorn	46
The Timpani	49
The Cymbals	50
The Side Drum	51
The Bass Drum	52
The Tum Drum	53
The Tubular Bells	54
The Triangle	55
The Xylophone	56
The Vibraphone	57
The Celeste	58
The Jingle Bells and the Chinese Block	59
The Wind Machine	60 & 61
The Gong and the Tam Tam	62
The Castanets	63